VOLCANO ATLAS

AN EPIC JOURNEY AROUND THE WORLD'S MOST INCREDIBLE VOLCANOES

Tom Jackson

Illustrations by Maggie Li

words&pictures

Author: Tom Jackson
Illustrator: Maggie Li
Editor: Nancy Dickmann
Designer: Karen Hood
Art Director: Susi Martin
Associate Publisher: Holly Willsher
Consultant: Priyanka Lamichhane

First published in 2024 by words & pictures,
an imprint of The Quarto Group.
100 Cummings Center,
Suite 265D Beverly,
MA 01915, USA.
T (978) 282-9590 F (978) 283-2742
www.quarto.com

A CIP record for this book is available
from the Library of Congress.

ISBN: 978-0-7112-8379-4

Printed in Malaysia COS052024

9 8 7 6 5 4 3 2 1

FSC
www.fsc.org
MIX
Paper | Supporting
responsible forestry
FSC® C007207

CONTENTS

Journey with us across the globe as we visit the largest, most powerful, and most dangerous volcanoes on the planet. Get ready for an awesome ride!

INTRODUCTION

A volcano is always an impressive sight. Many are towering cone-shaped mountains topped with snow and ice, where plumes of hot gas and clouds of choking smoke and ash billow out. A volcano literally has a hole in the top! This crater connects to Earth's hot interior, many thousands of feet below the surface. From time to time, the volcano erupts and hot lava and exploded rock fly out. The volcano is erupting.

There are about 1,350 active volcanoes, and up to 60 of them will erupt this year—but no one is quite sure which ones! Most eruptions are small displays of spurting lava and tall columns of smoke, but others are catastrophic events that destroy entire cities, blanket whole countries in a layer of ash, and change weather patterns across the globe.

Let's take a journey to the most amazing volcanoes around the world. Along the way, we will see lakes of lava, ice chimneys, and craters that could swallow a city. Are you ready to go volcano hunting? Let's do it!

THE RING OF FIRE

On Earth, more than one-third of all volcanoes on land—over 450 of them— are located in a loop around the edges of the Pacific Ocean. This part of the world is called the Ring of Fire, and it includes many of the world's largest and most violent volcanoes. The Ring of Fire exists due to the amount of movement of tectonic plates in the area. This pressure deep underground is what makes volcanoes form.

LARGEST VOLCANO?

One place we won't visit is the largest volcano ever seen. That's because Olympus Mons is not on Earth—it's on Mars! At 15.5 miles (25 kilometres) high, this volcano is almost three times taller than Mount Everest, and if it were on Earth, it would cover the width of France. Olympus Mons is so large because it is very old. Earth's surface shifts all the time, so volcanoes here don't last long enough to reach this size.

MARS

UNDERSEA VOLCANOES

The volcanoes we will visit are all on land, but there are another million on the seabed. Most of these volcanoes are extinct, which means they have stopped erupting. Scientists believe that 80 percent of the volcanic eruptions on Earth take place in the ocean. Many undersea volcanoes are tall, but these "seamounts" are hidden in the deep water.

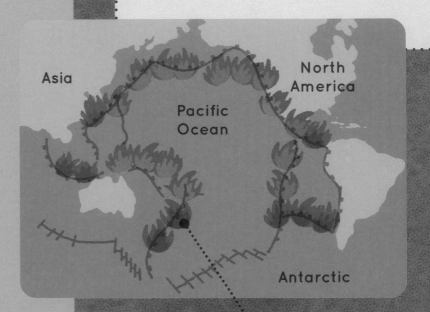

Asia

Pacific Ocean

North America

Antarctic

Ring of Fire

Olympus Mons

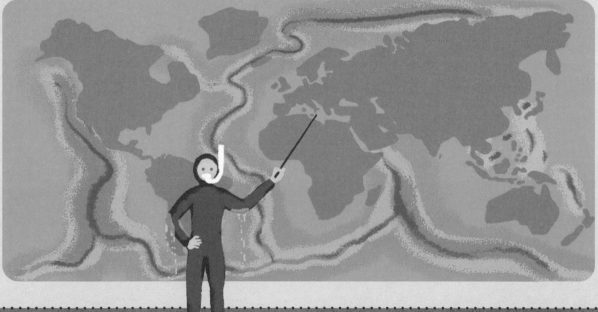

Most of the world's undersea volcanoes form mountain ranges on the seabed, along cracks or gaps in Earth's surface. Hot liquid rock called magma leaks out through these cracks, then cools into solid areas of new seabed.

FLOOD BASALTS

Surprisingly, the largest eruptions on Earth don't come from mountains. In a flood basalt eruption, lava gushes out of a long crack in Earth's surface, forming a deep lava sea that covers the land. The lava eventually cools into thick layers of rock called "traps." The Siberian Traps in Russia were formed 250 million years ago by an enormous eruption that lasted for centuries and spread lava over an area almost the size of Argentina! The Siberian Traps are thought to be the main cause of a mass extinction that killed 96 percent of all life on Earth.

Arctic Ocean

Russia

Siberian Traps

HOW VOLCANOES FORM

Earth's outer layer is a thin crust of solid rock. But this crust is not a single piece surrounding the whole planet—it is broken into dozens of chunks, called plates. The plates of hard rock sit on top of hotter, softer material underneath. Deeper still, the rocks melt into seething hot magma. Volcanoes form around the boundaries between plates, where the liquid magma is able to leak out and reach the surface.

Volcanoes are often tall mountains with a hole, or crater, at the top. This is where eruptions happen. Once magma leaves the volcano, we call it lava. The lava flows away from the crater, cooling as it goes until it forms a new layer of rock. Each eruption produces a new rock layer, making the mountain grow taller and taller.

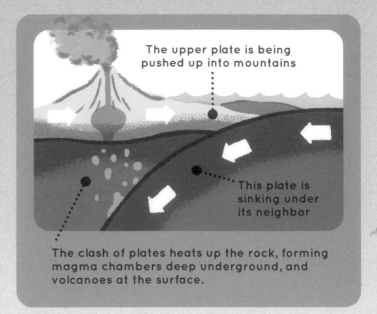

The upper plate is being pushed up into mountains

This plate is sinking under its neighbor

The clash of plates heats up the rock, forming magma chambers deep underground, and volcanoes at the surface.

A CRACK IN THE CRUST

A volcano forms where there is a crack in Earth's crust. This crack is so deep that it reaches a place where rock has melted into a red-hot, thick liquid called magma. Every now and then, the magma surges up through the crack to the surface and causes a volcanic eruption. Stay out of the way!

TYPES OF LAVA

Magma and lava are the same stuff—molten rock. But while magma stays underground, where Earth's heat keeps it mostly liquid, lava exists above the surface and is always cooling down to become solid rock. Lava that erupts underwater cools down very quickly and forms round blobs of rock on the seabed, called pillow lava. In the air, lava takes longer to cool. It can spurt into the air as a fiery fountain or flow over the land as rivers of melted rock. There are two main types of lava flow. Pahoehoe (pah hoey hoey) is runny lava that gushes quickly down a mountain. A'a (ah ah) is thick and crusty. It moves slowly and is often covered in a layer of chunky rocks.

Pillow lava

Pahoehoe lava

A'a lava

Crater

Ash cloud

Vents

Lava

Conduit

Magma
chamber

Magma

INSIDE A VOLCANO

Every volcano is unique, but they share
several main features. Deep underneath
is a magma chamber. This is connected by
a natural pipe or conduit to the vent—the
hole at the surface where eruptions occur.
The vent often forms a crater with steep
walls around the edge. Big volcanoes
can have several vents.

VOLCANO STATUS

Experts describe volcanoes in three ways:
active, dormant, and extinct. An active volcano
is one that is very likely to erupt again. It
might erupt tomorrow or in 100 years, but the
next eruption is coming. A dormant volcano is
not erupting now, but it could erupt at some
point in the future. The magma chamber
beneath contains sticky, thick magma, so
it is unlikely to erupt soon. However, if the
chamber fills up, or heats up a lot, the volcano
could become active once more. An extinct
volcano will never erupt again. Its magma
chamber may have emptied out and collapsed,
or its conduit is no longer connected to a
source of magma.

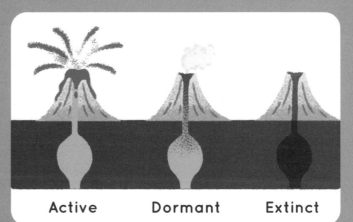

Active   Dormant   Extinct

TYPES OF VOLCANOES

No two volcanoes are the same. They all have a unique set of features that depends on how and where they formed. However, scientists have identified three main types of volcano, but there are many more volcanic formations. Mostly what defines each type is what comes out of the crater—and how fast—because different eruptions build volcanoes in different ways.

CINDER CONES

These are the simplest type of volcanoes, usually less than 1,000 feet (300 meters) tall. These steep-sided volcanoes formed from fragments of lava that were flung out of the crater. The cones are often made from sharp grains of dark material. A cinder cone often has an area of dark rocks around the base because lava flows out from vents near the bottom.

SHIELD VOLCANOES

Although these volcanoes are not always tall, they take up huge amounts of space, making them the biggest volcanoes on Earth. A shield volcano has a large crater at the summit, with the rest of the mountain forming a sloping oval around it. From above, this looks like a soldier's shield. Shield volcanoes form from layer after layer of runny lava that erupts slowly and spreads out in all directions.

TYPES OF ERUPTIONS

There are six main types of volcanic eruptions. Most are named after a real volcano or a part of the world where these eruptions are common. An eruption's type depends on what is being erupted—lava, ash, or perhaps a mixture of both—and how fast it happens. Some eruptions last for centuries, while others only take a minute.

VULCANIAN: A small eruption where gas builds up under the crater and then suddenly bursts out as a cloud of ash.

PELÉAN: An explosive eruption with a pyroclastic flow (a burst of hot ash and shattered pieces of rock) that flows quickly downhill.

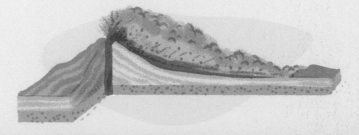

ERUPTION SIZE

Volcanic eruptions are measured using the Volcano Explosivity Index, or VEI for short. This scale runs from 0 to 8 and measures how much material is thrown out during an eruption. A VEI 1 eruption releases 3.5 million cubic ft (about 100,000 cubic m)—enough to fill London's Royal Albert Hall. A VEI 8 eruption releases enough to fill Lake Erie, twice over!

STRATOVOLCANOES

These volcanoes are also called composite volcanoes because they are made by many kinds of processes, including the ones that make cinder cones and shield volcanoes. They are the tallest and steepest of all volcanoes, some reaching more than 20,000 ft (6,000 m). These cone-shaped mountains are made from a mix of lava and ash layers.

LAVA DOMES

When huge masses of lava are too thick to travel far from the vent, it creates a lava dome. It becomes solid close to the crater, making a round dome-shaped mountain. The outer layers of lava domes are quite weak and frequently crumble away.

CALDERAS

This very large crater forms when a volcano erupts and collapses. Calderas are not huge peaks that are easy to spot—they may even be hidden by a lake or forest. However, if a caldera is still active there will be hot springs, geysers and other signs. Lakes often form in the depression.

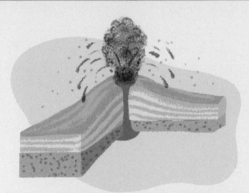

STROMBOLIAN: A small eruption where lava and ash spurt out of the crater, which can continue for many years.

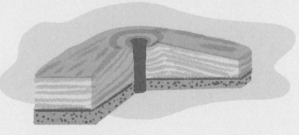

HAWAI'IAN: A slow eruption that produces large amounts of hot, runny lava.

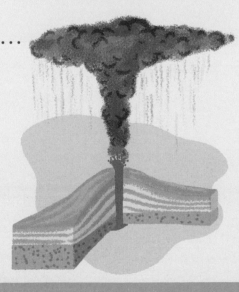

PLINIAN: An eruption that produces a huge billowing cloud of ash, caused by magma mixing with gases and steam.

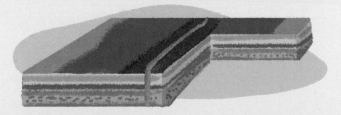

ICELANDIC: A slow eruption similar to the Hawai'ian type but where the lava erupts along a crack on the ground instead of from a mountain crater.

VOLCANIC FEATURES

There is a lot more to volcanoes than craters and cone-shaped mountains. Flowing lava creates some interesting structures that become solid parts of the landscape. But even more features are created when water trickling through the ground in volcanic areas is heated. This creates a hydrothermal system, which can include features such as natural fountains, hot springs, and boiling mud!

TUBES AND CHIMNEYS

After an eruption, explorers may find empty tunnels or "tubes" running under the surface. These lava tubes form when lava flows into a natural channel, perhaps one left by a previous eruption. The top of the lava cools into a solid crust, but deeper down it stays hot enough to keep flowing. Once it's out, the empty tube remains. The Kazumura lava tube system in Hawai'i is 40 mi (65 km) long!

Fumaroles are like little chimneys made from minerals. They form where hot steam and other gases escape from a crack in the ground. As the steam cools, some of the chemicals mixed in it will turn into solid crystals. Gradually these crystals build up, forming a tall chimney or spout.

DEEP-SEA VENTS

When seawater seeps into the rocks of the seabed in volcanic areas, it becomes extremely hot. Deep under the sea the pressure is so high that the water can't boil, so it gushes out of holes in the seabed. These are called hydrothermal vents. The hot water immediately cools down because it mixes with the cool seawater, and the chemicals mixed into it form a dark smokelike cloud of tiny grains. Bacteria living around the vents eat these chemicals, and many unusual animals live beside the vents to feed on the bacteria.

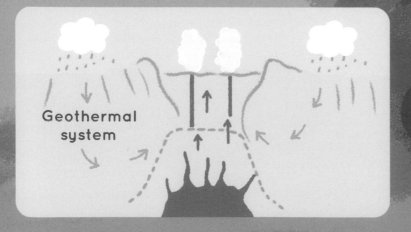

Geothermal system

HOT SPRINGS

When volcanically heated water reaches the surface, it is still too hot for most life to survive in it. However, there are some species of bacteria and other microbes that are able to survive temperatures that would cook other organisms! These "thermophiles" can often turn the hydrothermal water an unusual color.

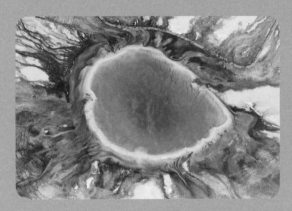

The hot water in hydrothermal systems does things that cold water cannot. The heat has enough energy to dissolve more minerals from the rocks and alter their chemical makeup. As it cools toward the surface, the water releases the minerals, which then turn back into crystals. This is why volcanic areas have large amounts of gems and metals like silver and gold.

Geysers are natural fountains that are a complicated type of hot spring. The hot water is contained in chambers deep underground. Every now and then the conditions are right for the boiling water to flow up to the surface, rushing out of a spout to shoot high into the air and make a cloud of droplets. Some geysers go off every few minutes, while others stay quiet for decades. Old Faithful, a geyser in Yellowstone National Park in the United States, gets its name because it puts on a display every hour or so, without fail.

MUD POTS

These areas are filled with bubbling mud. This is because the hot water deeper down is boiling into steam, which then bubbles up through gooey, dangerous mud. The mud is easily hot enough to kill, and smells like rotten eggs due to the presence of the mineral sulfur.

VESUVIUS

Vesuvius is a stratovolcano on the western coast of Italy, near the modern city of Naples. It is still active and erupted as recently as 1944, but it is most famous for an eruption in 79 CE. This disaster completely buried the Roman city of Pompeii and several nearby towns. A cloud of super-hot ash and gas called a pyroclastic flow surged down the side of the mountain. It covered Pompeii—and everyone in it—in a heavy blanket of ash in a matter of minutes. For centuries, the city lay forgotten under a thick layer of volcanic ash, until it was dug up again many centuries later.

Italy

NAME: VESUVIUS

COUNTRY: ITALY

TYPE: STRATOVOLCANO

HEIGHT: 4,203 FT (1,281 M)

LAST ERUPTION: 1944

NUMBER OF KNOWN ERUPTIONS: MORE THAN 50

BIGGEST ERUPTION: 79 CE

PEOPLE LIVING WITHIN 20 MI: MORE THAN 2 MILLION

CLAIM TO FAME: BURIED THE ROMAN CITY OF POMPEII UNDER ASH

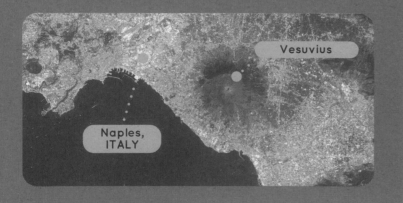

Vesuvius

Naples, ITALY

PYROCLASTIC FLOW

These kinds of flows are one of the most deadly features of some types of volcanic eruption. They happen when a volcano spews out hot gases, ash, and solidified pieces of lava. This heavy, choking cloud plunges downhill and can reach speeds of more than 435 miles per hour (700 kilometers per hour). The cloud can reach 1,300° Fahrenheit (700° Celsius) and instantly kills all in its path.

A SLOW START

The deadly eruption of Vesuvius in 79 CE started gradually. Small earthquakes began a few days before the eruption—often a sign that a volcano is becoming more active. The eruption began around midday on August 24, when a tall ash cloud appeared above the mountain. A few hours later, ash began to fall like snow on the streets of Pompeii, and the air was noticeably warmer. Many people decided to leave Pompeii around this time. It is thought that of the 11,000 people living there, around 9,000 escaped.

FROZEN IN TIME

Pompeii was frozen in time by the hot volcanic ash. The city's houses and streets were buried, as were the people and animals. The ash hardened and locked everything in place. Eventually, the dead bodies rotted away, leaving a hollow space behind. Centuries later, archaeologists filled the hollows with plaster, creating lifelike casts of the people killed in the eruption.

THE SITUATION WORSENS

By the next morning, the roofs of houses were beginning to collapse under the weight of the ash. Even worse, the mountain started blasting rocks into the sky. Escaping was now much harder. In the middle of the night, the deadly pyroclastic flow emerged from the crater and rushed toward Pompeii. It took less than fifteen minutes to reach the city and smother it.

PLINY AND PLINY The best account of the 79 CE eruption of Vesuvius was made by the Roman writer Pliny the Younger, who watched from his uncle's home farther along the coast. This uncle, known as Pliny the Elder, was a military commander as well as a scientist and writer. When the eruption began, Pliny the Elder sent a fleet of ships to rescue people. He traveled with them but was suffocated by the hot dust and gas once on shore.

SANTORINI

This horseshoe-shaped Greek island—also known as Thira—is part of the remains of a huge volcanic crater called a caldera, which is now filled with seawater. But about 3,600 years ago, the island looked completely different. There was a mountain where the caldera is today! It was blown apart after an enormous eruption that is said to have wiped out an entire civilization. Legend has it that the eruption even sank an entire city beneath the waves!

NAME: SANTORINI

COUNTRY: GREECE

TYPE: SHIELD

HEIGHT: 1,204 FT (367 M)

LAST ERUPTION: 1950

NUMBER OF KNOWN ERUPTIONS: 12

BIGGEST ERUPTION: 1620 BCE

PEOPLE LIVING WITHIN 20 MI: 15,500

CLAIM TO FAME: MAY HAVE DESTROYED THE LEGENDARY CITY OF ATLANTIS

Greece

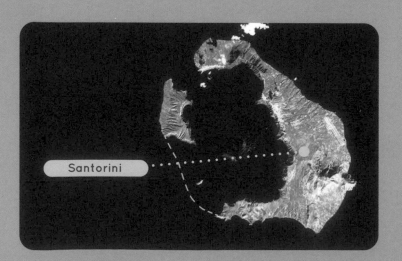

Santorini

IS THIS ATLANTIS? Greek legends tell of the city of Atlantis, a place known for its clever and wealthy citizens. The stories say that it was lost below the waves in a great disaster, never to be seen again. Historians think that the legend could actually be the true story of the eruption of Santorini. They have already found the ruins of one ancient city on Thira, buried under volcanic ash. Perhaps there was another city on the island that simply fell into the sea!

A BIG BLAST

The eruption of Santorini happened sometime around 1620 BCE. It was one of the biggest eruptions ever, sending up to 19 cubic mi (80 cubic km) of rock 25 mi (40 km) into the sky. That's like throwing 3,000 Great Pyramids almost halfway to space! The eruption left a very big hole deep under the seabed and most of the island fell into it, leaving the bay that we see today.

SPREADING FAR AND WIDE

The cloud of ash and dust would have spread around the world, blocking out the Sun and making it dark and cold. There were no eyewitness accounts of the eruption, but a carving from ancient Egypt tells the story of the country being hit by a huge storm with dark clouds and powerful lightning—possibly coming across the sea from Santorini. Chinese history records that the weather was so cold around this time that the ground was still frozen in summer.

WASHED AWAY The most powerful people in the area were the Minoans, who lived on the island of Crete. According to legend, their king kept a monstrous half-man half-bull called the Minotaur trapped in a mazelike labyrinth in his palace. The eruption of Santorini would have created a tsunami that smashed into Crete, damaging coastal towns and cities and perhaps destroying the Minoans' ships. The Minoan civilization faded away soon after.

THE VOLCANO TODAY

The caldera deep beneath the island of Thira is still volcanically active. It gradually fills with magma and erupts from time to time. There was a big submarine eruption in 1650, and in the last few centuries there have been several small ones and some bigger ones on the nearby seabed. Today there are two little volcanic islands in the middle of the caldera, made by lava building up from the seabed. Santorini will erupt again!

ETNA

This giant volcano looms high above the island of Sicily in the far south of Italy. It sits above the place where the African and Eurasian plates meet, deep beneath the Mediterranean Sea. Etna, which means "furnace" in the ancient Phoenician language, has been erupting every few years for centuries. Even so, the island is heavily populated, with many towns and two large cities. Scientists at the Etna Observatory watch for eruptions. The volcano normally produces slow-moving lava, and if it looks like the flows are heading toward a town, experts create barriers and dig artificial channels to divert it.

ETNA IN ACTION

There has been volcanic activity in this region for about 500,000 years, and much of the eastern coast of Sicily was created by volcanic eruptions. About 8,000 years ago, a large part of Etna's eastern slope fell into the sea and caused a tsunami. The volcano's height is always changing as new eruptions add more lava to the summit. However, these new rock formations can also collapse or be pushed away by the next eruption. The entire mountain is on the move, shifting an inch or so toward the sea each year, as the upper rocks slide down a deeper sloping layer.

NAME: ETNA

COUNTRY: ITALY

TYPE: STRATOVOLCANO

HEIGHT: 11,014 FT (3,357 M)

LAST ERUPTION: 2022

NUMBER OF KNOWN ERUPTIONS: 200

BIGGEST ERUPTION: 1500 BCE

PEOPLE LIVING WITHIN 20 MI: 1 MILLION

CLAIM TO FAME: MOST ACTIVE VOLCANO IN EUROPE

Italy

MONSTER'S LAIR According to Greek mythology, Zeus, the king of the gods, imprisoned the monstrous flying snake Typhon under the mountain after a battle for control of the universe. Fire-breathing Typhon has been trying to escape ever since, causing the volcanic eruptions and earthquakes.

Stromboli

Vulcano

Sicily, ITALY

Mount Etna

VULCANO

Another of the Aeolian islands is called Vulcano, and is the site of a small volcano about 1,640 ft (500 m) high, which last erupted in 1890. The name of this volcano is where we get our modern word "volcano." The mountain is named after Vulcan, the Roman god of fire. According to Roman mythology, the mountain was a chimney for the forge deep underground where Vulcan worked as a blacksmith for the gods.

STROMBOLI

North of Sicily are the volcanic Aeolian Islands, named for the Greek god of the wind. There are several volcanoes here, all sitting above the same plate boundary as Etna. Most of the volcanoes are dormant, but those on the island of Stromboli are highly active. There have been small eruptions of ash, gases, and chunks of hot rocks there almost every day for at least the last 2,000 years! Because its constant eruptions can be seen from far away, it is nicknamed "the lighthouse of the Mediterranean."

EYJAFJALLAJÖKULL

This mountain in Iceland is part icecap, part volcano, with the volcano itself lying beneath the glacier. It's a rather quiet volcano, with only a few small eruptions over the last 1,000 years or so. The last one was in 2010, and while it wasn't huge, it certainly got a lot of attention! The eruption spewed out a vast ash cloud that was too dangerous to fly through, so ten million people had their flights canceled!

Iceland

NAME: EYJAFJALLAJÖKULL

COUNTRY: ICELAND

TYPE: STRATOVOLCANO

HEIGHT: 5,417 FT (1,651 M)

LAST ERUPTION: 2010

NUMBER OF KNOWN ERUPTIONS: 5

BIGGEST ERUPTION: 2010

PEOPLE LIVING WITHIN 20 MI: OVER 700

CLAIM TO FAME: CREATED AN ASH CLOUD THAT STOPPED PLANES FROM FLYING ACROSS EUROPE

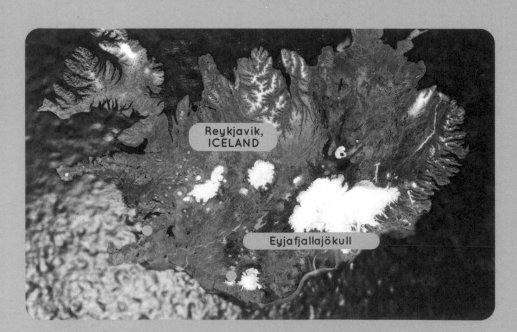

Reykjavik, ICELAND

Eyjafjallajökull

A BIG CLOUD

The Eyjafjallajökull eruption started with lava erupting down the side of the mountain. Some lava flowed into a nearby river, making the water almost hot enough to make a cup of tea! The lava also melted ice on the mountainsides, creating flood water that gushed down to the sea.

ASH CLOUD DANGER

Volcanic ash clouds are made up of tiny particles of rock released during an eruption. The tiny specks are so sharp that if a plane flies through the cloud, the dust will scrape off the paint and scratch the windows! The dust also gets sucked into the hot jet engines, where it melts and forms a coating of glass. That coating makes the engine seize up—never a good thing! Air traffic controllers are careful to divert planes around ash clouds. Most of these clouds are very high, far above where planes fly.

HERE COMES TROUBLE

In the next stage, the volcano began to erupt under the thick cap of ice on top of the mountain. The mix of hot lava, exploding rock, and cold ice created a vast cloud of steam and very fine grains of dust. This ash cloud rose over 6 mi (9 km) into the sky, which is low for a volcanic eruption. At this height the cloud caught the wind and spread over western Europe.

SURTSEY

In the 1960s, out to sea a little south of Eyjafjallajökull, Icelanders could watch as a brand new island was being made. Over a period of four years, an undersea volcanic eruption created a new island called Surtsey. The crumbly rocks of this island are being gradually washed away by the sea. No humans are allowed on the island other than a few scientists who are watching it closely to learn more about how wildlife arrives and takes over new land.

LAND OF ICE AND FIRE Iceland lies just below the Arctic Circle and is covered in snow for a lot of the year. However, Iceland has fire as well as ice, with 130 volcanoes—35 of which are active. The island sits on an immense crack in Earth's crust, called the Mid-Atlantic Ridge, which runs from the Arctic all the way through the Atlantic Ocean to the Antarctic. There are volcanoes all the way along this crack, but most are deep underwater. Iceland is one of the few places where they rise out of the sea.

PICO DEL TEIDE

This triangular mountain in Tenerife is the highest point in the Canary Islands, a group of Spanish islands off the coast of North Africa. It's also the highest point in the whole of the Atlantic Ocean. At dawn and dusk, the mighty peak casts one of the world's longest shadows, stretching for 25 mi (40 km) and touching two of the other islands. The mountain's name comes from an old word for Hell, because ancient people believed a demon inside it was trying to steal the Sun. So far he's failed!

NAME: PICO DEL TEIDE

COUNTRY: SPAIN

TYPE: STRATOVOLCANO

HEIGHT: 12,198 FT (3,718 M)

LAST ERUPTION: 1909

NUMBER OF KNOWN ERUPTIONS: 42

BIGGEST ERUPTION: 80 BCE

PEOPLE LIVING WITHIN 20 MI: OVER 300,000

CLAIM TO FAME: THE HIGHEST POINT IN THE ATLANTIC OCEAN

Tenerife

Pico del Teide

CANARY ISLANDS

HOLDING UP THE SKY

The ancient Guanches people lived on Tenerife before the Spanish took over in 1496. The Guanches believed that the mountain held up the sky and was the home of a demon named Guayota, who sometimes took the form of a black dog. Guayota had once kidnapped the Sun, turning the world dark. This myth might be referring to a big eruption many centuries ago. According to legend, the people were saved by the god Achamán, who imprisoned the monster inside the volcano and released the Sun.

A COMPLEX MOUNTAIN

Pico del Teide is a complex volcano, with a top cone that sits inside a huge crater left behind by a much older volcano. Teide is still active but has not erupted for more than 100 years. However, it has been erupting every few centuries for thousands of years. It is being watched especially closely because a big eruption here could be very destructive for the people living on the islands.

A GOOD VIEW

All kinds of explorers come to Pico de Teide! One of the world's leading astronomical observatories is located here. The weather conditions are ideal for looking deep into space. The sky is often clear and the air is still, which reduces the twinkle of the starlight.

MEGATSUNAMI

Cumbre Vieja on the island of La Palma is another active volcano in the Canary Islands. Its frequent eruptions spew out lava and set forests on fire. A group of volcanologists once suggested that when the volcano runs out of magma, the entire mountain could crack. If this were to happen, one half would slide into the ocean. That would create a "megatsunami"—a wall of water hundreds of yards high that would surge across the Atlantic, smashing into the coasts of North and South America. It sounds terrifying and amazing all at once! However, more recent research suggests that La Palma is unlikely to fall apart in this way and even if it did, the waves it caused would be much smaller.

ERTA ALE

This volcano in the deserts of northern Ethiopia is one of the most unusual volcanoes on Earth. Although its name means "smoking mountain," it is not tall—only about 1,970 ft (600) from base to peak. And its base is actually more than 330 ft (100 m) below sea level! That's because the whole mountain is inside a giant depression in Earth's surface. Erta Ale is about 30 mi (50 km) wide, built up from layer after layer of the lava that erupts almost continuously from its crater. The crater has a lake of red-hot lava inside!

NAME: ERTA ALE

COUNTRY: ETHIOPIA

TYPE: SHIELD

HEIGHT: OVER 1,970 FT (600 M)

LAST ERUPTION: CONTINUOUSLY ERUPTING SINCE 1967

NUMBER OF KNOWN ERUPTIONS: 4

BIGGEST ERUPTION: NOW

PEOPLE LIVING WITHIN 20 MI: OVER 8,800

CLAIM TO FAME: THE CRATER HAS A PERMANENT LAKE OF LAVA

Ethiopia

Erta Ale

ARABIAN PENINSULA

ETHIOPIA

THE GREAT RIFT VALLEY

Erta Ale is located in the Great Rift Valley, which is a wide crack that runs down from the Middle East, through the Red Sea and into eastern Africa. The rift is formed by neighboring plates of Earth's crust that are slowly moving apart from each other. This movement creates deep depressions and a lot of volcanoes. Millions of years from now, the Great Rift Valley could be flooded by a brand new sea, and eastern Africa could become an island.

A LAKE OF LAVA

Erta Ale has been erupting continuously for more than fifty years but there has been a permanent lake of lava in its crater since at least 1906. It is one of only eight volcanoes in the world with a permanent lava lake, and none have lasted as long as Erta Ale's.

THE DANAKIL DEPRESSION

Erta Ale is in a region called the Danakil Depression, one of the lowest and hottest places on Earth. The depression is surrounded by hills on three sides and joins the Great Rift Valley to the south. Here, three separate plates are pulling apart to create a low-lying hollow where the crust is always on the move. As well as volcanoes, the Danakil Depression also has hot springs, where water warmed by underground magma bubbles up to the surface. As the water turns to steam it leaves behind minerals, which form colorful crusts around the pools.

LOOK BUT DON'T TOUCH!

When the volcano is quiet, the top of the lake is sometimes covered with a thin skin of dark rock, but the currents of lava underneath are always creating fresh cracks and churning up this crust. The lava lake is deep, going all the way down to a magma chamber several thousand yards underground. Don't get too close—it could spurt out a fountain of molten rock at any second!

CRADLE OF LIFE The Awash River flows into the Danakil Depression but never reaches the sea, forming a string of salty lakes instead. Fossil remains of our earliest human ancestors have been found in this region. "Lucy" is one of these, an early ape ancestor who lived more than three million years ago and could walk on two legs. Her bones were dug up near the Awash River.

23

KILIMANJARO

This African volcano is a record-breaker in many ways: Kilimanjaro is not only Africa's biggest volcano—it is the highest volcano in the Eastern Hemisphere. Kilimanjaro is also Africa's tallest mountain of any kind. It is about three-quarters the height of Mount Everest and people can hike to the top without the need for specialist climbing equipment, but they would need to train and prepare first! Kilimanjaro is technically an active volcano, but it has not erupted for at least 150,000 years.

NAME: KILIMANJARO

COUNTRY: TANZANIA

TYPE: STRATOVOLCANO

HEIGHT: 19,295 FT (5,881 M)

LAST ERUPTION:
OVER 150,000 YEARS AGO

NUMBER OF KNOWN ERUPTIONS:
UNKNOWN

BIGGEST ERUPTION: UNKNOWN

PEOPLE LIVING WITHIN 20 MI: 298,129

CLAIM TO FAME: TALLEST MOUNTAIN IN AFRICA

Tanzania

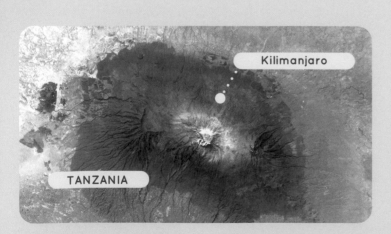

Kilimanjaro

TANZANIA

THREE IN ONE

Kilimanjaro is actually three volcanoes in one. The two slightly lower craters, called Shira and Mawenzi, are extinct. Scientists think that the taller one, Kibo, is only dormant. There are few records of Kibo's activity in the past but it is thought that around 200 years ago some

Shira

STANDING FREE

Kilimanjaro is the world's tallest free-standing mountain, which means that it is not part of a mountain range. It just rises up out of a flat plain spreading out in all directions. Because of this, the distance from its base to its peak—16,076 ft (4,900 m) —is greater than that of any other mountain, even Everest. Tall mountains like Everest are normally surrounded by foothills and small peaks, but Kilimanjaro is not. Instead, it is surrounded by savanna.

fumaroles in this crater gave out smoke and gases. Kilimanjaro has been quiet since then, but for how much longer?

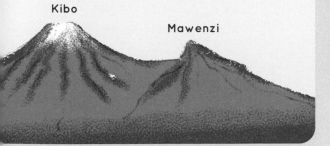

Kibo

Mawenzi

MELTING GLACIERS

Kilimanjaro is near the Equator, where it is hot all year round. However, the top of the mountain is above the snowline, where it is always below freezing. Some areas of the summit are covered with ice, but these glaciers are getting steadily smaller due to climate change. More than 80 percent of the ice has melted away in the last century, and there will likely be no more ice on Kilimanjaro by 2050.

CLIMATE ZONES A climber walking up Kilimanjaro will pass through a series of climate zones. The zones begin on the hot East African savanna, but above 5,900 ft (1,800 m) the grasslands and shrubs give way to rainforest. Above 9,200 ft (2,800 m) the air continues to get cooler and there is less moisture, so a moorland of grasses and heather grows here. Above 13,000 ft (4,000 m), temperatures drop below freezing at night so only small alpine plants cling on. At the very top the mountain is covered in ice.

BUSY NEIGHBORS

On the other side of the Great Rift Valley there are two very active volcanoes, both in the Democratic Republic of the Congo. Mount Nyamulagira is Africa's most active volcano, erupting more than forty times in the last hundred years. Nearby is Mount Nyiragongo, which is the second-most active volcano in Africa, which has been erupting continuously for twenty years! It has the deepest lava lake in the world, with walls that plunge 820 ft (250 m) into a crater. Its lava flows faster than any other volcano's, rushing down the mountain at speeds of about 35 miles (60 km) per hour!

PITON DE LA FOURNAISE

This enormous volcano, which forms the lower third of the Indian Ocean island of Réunion, is one of the world's most active volcanoes. It has erupted twenty-nine times since the start of the century, which is more than once a year! Its French name means "peak of the furnace," and the top of the mountain has several craters inside a much bigger caldera. The caldera is 5 mi (8 km) wide and is called the Enclos Fouqué, or "ring of craziness."

Réunion

NAME: PITON DE LA FOURNAISE

COUNTRY: FRANCE (RÉUNION)

TYPE: SHIELD

HEIGHT: 8,635 FT (2,632 M)

LAST ERUPTION: 2023

NUMBER OF KNOWN ERUPTIONS: 197

BIGGEST ERUPTION: 2765 BCE

PEOPLE LIVING WITHIN 20 MI: OVER 240,000

CLAIM TO FAME: TURNS BEACHES ON THE ISLAND GREEN!

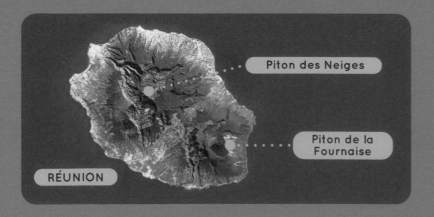

Piton des Neiges

Piton de la Fournaise

RÉUNION

TOURIST ATTRACTION

As volcanoes go, Piton de la Fournaise is very active but not very violent, so it is a great place for tourists to watch a volcano in action. There are walking paths up above the caldera that lead to viewpoints where people can look down at eruptions from a safe distance. The eruptions of lava are nearly always contained within the caldera, and any lava that escapes flows down the eastern slopes, plunging into the Indian Ocean.

THE GREAT BURN

Most of Piton de la Fournaise's eruptions come from two craters called Bory and Dolomieu. Most of the caldera has high cliff walls, but the eastern side of the caldera is open. The lava floods out here and down the mountainside to the Indian Ocean. With regular eruptions, this area is frequently coated with hot lava, so it is known as the "Great Burn." Between eruptions, fast-growing shrubs sprout, and there are also scarred areas of scorched earth that shows where lava flowed before. The coastal road that runs through the Great Burn is often blocked by lava.

GREEN BEACHES

The lava from Piton de la Fournaise contains a large amount of a green mineral called olivine. As the lava flows down the Great Burn, it cools into solid rocks and crystals. Over time, rain and wind break up the lava. The grains of olivine are washed down the mountain to the beach, where they make the sand green!

PITON DES NEIGES

Réunion has a larger volcano, Piton des Neiges ("Snow Peak"), which fills much of the center of the island. Although now probably extinct, this mountain is still taller than Piton de la Fournaise. Most of the old craters have now collapsed, forming deep, rugged valleys. Some of these remote places were used in the nineteenth century by escaped enslaved people to hide from the authorities.

RAIN RECORDS

Commerson Crater outside the Enclos Fouqué has a strange microclimate. When tropical storms hit the island, the rain clouds gather over this crater and drop a huge amount of rain. In 1980 21 ft (6.5 m) of rain fell into the crater in just fifteen days—a world record! The crater also earned another record for heavy rainfall in 2007, when 155 inches (3,929 millimeters) of rain fell during a single 72-hour storm.

BIG BEN

This volcano is Australia's highest mountain, although it is closer to Antarctica than to the rest of Australia! It's located on Heard Island, part of an Australian territory in the icy Southern Ocean. Seal hunters lived here in the 1860s and 70s, but once they had killed most of the seals, they left. No one lives there now. The first recorded eruption from Big Ben was in 1881, and since then there have been twelve more.

NAME: BIG BEN

COUNTRY: AUSTRALIA (HEARD ISLAND)

TYPE: STRATOVOLCANO

HEIGHT: 9,006 FT (2,745 M)

LAST ERUPTION: CONTINUOUSLY ERUPTING SINCE 2012

NUMBER OF KNOWN ERUPTIONS: 13

BIGGEST ERUPTION: 1985

PEOPLE LIVING WITHIN 20 MI: 0

CLAIM TO FAME: TALLEST MOUNTAIN IN AUSTRALIAN TERRITORY

Heard Island

HEARD ISLAND

Big Ben

HARD TO REACH

Heard Island is one of Earth's most remote places. The island is located about 2,547 mi (4,099 km) southwest of Perth, Australia, and about the same distance from South Africa in the other direction. The volcano is actually slightly closer to Madagascar. Antarctica lies 1,013 mi (1,620 km) to the south—about the same distance as from London to the Arctic Circle! Although helicopters have managed to land here, most people get from Australia to Heard Island by ship. It's a two-week voyage through cold, treacherous waters.

KEEPING BUSY

It may be one of the most remote volcanoes in the world, but Big Ben is quite active. The volcano has been erupting continuously for the last ten years! Today, scientists keep an eye on it by using satellites that look to see how hot the crater is as they fly over.

BIG AND SMALL

There is actually one other volcano. Mount Dixon is much smaller than Big Ben and is located a few miles to the west, next to Atlas Cove. This is where visiting ships anchor and set up camp. This whole area of the seabed is called the Kerguelen Plateau, and while there are other volcanic islands in the area, none are as tall and active as Big Ben.

ELEPHANT SPIT

On the eastern shore of Heard Island is Elephant Spit, a long sandbank that stretches out 6 mi (9 km) into the sea. It was formed by the action of the glaciers that cover Big Ben. These rivers of ice grind away at the volcanic rocks beneath, turning them into pebbles and grains that are washed out to sea. On a map, the spit looks like an elephant's trunk, but it got its name because the area was once a haven for elephant seals. These huge sea mammals came to Elephant Spit to breed.

NATURAL ECOSYSTEM

The wildlife on Heard Island is special because no non-native species have survived there. Normally mice, rats, and other animals are introduced wherever people visit, but this has not happened here. This makes Heard Island a good place for scientists to learn about the region's ecosystems. However, in recent years, new plants have appeared on the island. Their seeds may have arrived in the droppings of seabirds flying from other islands, or maybe they were stuck to the boot of a human visitor!

29

EREBUS

Located on the icebound Ross Islands, just off the coast of Antarctica, this is the world's southernmost active volcano. It began to form 1.3 million years ago and has been active for much of that time. The most recent eruption has been going on for the last fifty years. Erebus is currently one of the few volcanoes in the world with a lake of liquid lava in its crater. However, that does not stop the rest of the mountain from being covered in snow and ice!

NAME: EREBUS

CONTINENT: ANTARCTICA

TYPE: STRATOVOLCANO

HEIGHT: 12,448 FT (3,794 M)

LAST ERUPTION: 2023

NUMBER OF KNOWN ERUPTIONS: 20

BIGGEST ERUPTION: 1955

PEOPLE LIVING WITHIN 20 MI: 0

CLAIM TO FAME: THE WORLD'S SOUTHERNMOST VOLCANO

Antarctica

Ross Island, ANTARCTICA

Erebus

DARK NAME

Mount Erebus was named by James Clark Ross, a famous British polar explorer. He gave the volcano the name of his ship, HMS *Erebus*, which itself was named after the Greek god of darkness. Ross discovered the magnetic north pole in the 1830s and then headed south to explore the Antarctic. A lot of things in Antarctica are named after him! Ross Island, where Erebus is located, is surrounded by the Ross Sea, and the Ross Ice Shelf covers much of the sea.

QUIET PHASE

Erebus's current crater, which is 1,969 ft (600 m) wide and more than 361 ft (110 m) deep, was formed near the top of the mountain by a huge explosion about 18,000 years ago. Today, Mount Erebus erupts in a less violent way by releasing thick lava—as well as the occasional fountain of ash and lava bombs! The rock that forms from the cooled lava is called clinkstone because it makes a bell-like sound when two pieces are knocked together.

LONG-DISTANCE OBSERVERS

For many years, volcanologists visited Erebus each summer. They installed instruments to detect gases coming from the mountain and monitor for vibrations in the ground. These instruments sent information to the nearby research base at McMurdo Sound—this was then forwarded to researchers across the world. Today, Erebus's temperature and shape are watched by satellites in space.

ROBOT EXPLORER

Erebus's crater throws out clouds of poisonous sulfur dioxide gas, so it is much too dangerous for humans to explore. In 1992 scientists sent an eight-legged robot called Dante instead to collect gas samples. Linked to its controllers by a long wire, Dante managed to climb most of the way into the crater but didn't record any data. The mission wasn't a complete failure, however. It showed that robot explorers were a new way forward for gathering information from craters.

ICE FUMAROLES

Like many other volcanoes, Mount Erebus has tall chimney-like structures called fumaroles. Most fumaroles are formed from rocky minerals, which collect together where steam and hot gases burst out from a volcano's vents. Erebus's fumaroles are towers of ice! As the hot gases melt through the ice, they make steam, and this refreezes into ice that slowly builds up into a chimney. Bacteria live here, and scientists study them to learn more about how alien life might survive on cold ice worlds far out in space.

RUAPEHU

New Zealand is a land filled with volcanoes—there are twenty-four active ones and many more extinct craters. Mount Ruapehu is the biggest and one of the most active. It is the highest mountain on North Island, and its name means "exploding pit" in Māori, the language of the indigenous people of New Zealand. In the *Lord of the Rings* films, which were made in New Zealand, Mount Ruapehu starred as Mount Doom, a fiery mountain controlled by a wizard.

NAME: RUAPEHU

COUNTRY: NEW ZEALAND

TYPE: STRATOVOLCANO

HEIGHT: 9,177 FT (2,797 M)

LAST ERUPTION: 2007

NUMBER OF KNOWN ERUPTIONS: 64

BIGGEST ERUPTION: AROUND 7840 BCE

PEOPLE LIVING WITHIN 20 MI: OVER 6,500

CLAIM TO FAME: LARGEST VOLCANO IN NEW ZEALAND

New Zealand

Ruapehu

LAHARS

The summit of Mount Ruapehu is cold and covered in snow all year round. That means that the heat of eruptions can create dangerous events called lahars, where the snow and ice melt suddenly to create a torrent of mud and rock that gushes quickly downhill. Lahars from Ruapehu have added poisonous chemicals into river water, killing the fish that lived there. In 1953, a lahar washed away a railway bridge just as a train was crossing it, killing 151 people onboard.

LAKE TAUPO

North of Ruapehu is Lake Taupo, located in the crater of a supervolcano. This has had two confirmed eruptions—once 26,500 years ago and again about 1,800 years ago—but there may have been more. Both are among the largest eruptions ever to occur. Luckily, people were not yet living in New Zealand at the time of the second event, when water mixed with the lava to make a cloud of rock dust that settled in a deep layer across North Island. Heaps of rock and ash built up around the lake, making it larger and deeper. Eventually, the banks broke open and water flooded over the surrounding land.

THREE PEAKS AND A LAKE

Ruapehu has three peaks and the volcanic crater is nestled in between them. When it is not erupting, the crater is filled with water and is known as Crater Lake. The water in the lake is highly acidic due to the minerals dissolved in it from the surrounding rocks.

Mount Doom

VOLCANO SKIING

Mount Ruapehu is unusual for an active volcano because it has three ski resorts on its slopes. This is the biggest zone suitable for skiing in New Zealand. Much of the area is also prone to lahars, so there is an early warning system in place to clear the slopes before an eruption.

NEIGHBORS, NEW AND OLD

Ruapehu is a very active volcano, with about thirty eruptions in the last fifty years. It is thought to have started erupting 250,000 years ago, and so will have erupted many more times than that. To the west is Mount Hauhungatahi, which is nearly one million years old and long extinct. However, to the north is Mount Ngauruhoe, which is much younger at only 2,500 years old. It is competing with its much bigger neighbor to be the most active!

TAMBORA

The eruption of this Indonesian volcano in 1815 is said to be the largest in recorded history. Although the eruptions at Santorini and Taupo were bigger, no one was around to make records of what happened. Tambora's eruption took place at a time when scientists were learning more about volcanoes. When the mountain exploded it threw about 36 cubic mi (150 cubic km) of rock into the air. This tragically killed over 10,000 people and created food shortages that killed 100,000 more—and showed just how powerful and devastating volcanoes could be.

NAME: TAMBORA

COUNTRY: INDONESIA

TYPE: STRATOVOLCANO

HEIGHT: 9,350 FT (2,850 M)

LAST ERUPTION: 1967

NUMBER OF KNOWN ERUPTIONS: 7

BIGGEST ERUPTION: 1815

PEOPLE LIVING WITHIN 20 MI: OVER 89,000

CLAIM TO FAME: THE LARGEST VOLCANIC ERUPTION IN RECORDED HISTORY

Indonesia

Tambora

THE BUILD-UP

The volcano hadn't erupted for several centuries, but for the three years leading up to the 1815 eruption, it had been producing clouds of ash and occasional small explosions. Deep inside, the magma was building up to pressures that were 5,000 times stronger than atmospheric pressure. The temperature inside the volcano was around 1,500°F (800°C).

MANY BIG BANGS

On April 5, the mountain erupted with a thunderous bang. The next day, there was an even louder sound that was heard in Sumatra, 1,600 mi (2,600 km) away. By April 10, pyroclastic flows shot down the slopes, wiping out towns and villages. The mountain had been about 14,100 ft (4,300 m) tall before the eruption, but now it had lost roughly a third of its height. Around 11 billion tons of rock had been thrown out of the volcano, and much of it was being blown in the wind, spreading all over the world.

LOST CULTURE The people who lived in the jungle around the mountain were also called the Tambora, and all 10,000 of them were killed by the eruption. Archaeologists have explored the area, and buried under a thick layer of ash and dust they found houses and skeletons. The pottery and metalwork of the Tambora people show that they were well-off, but after the eruption, their land, culture, and language were completely lost.

GLOBAL IMPACT

A vast region was covered by a cloud of ash. Rain falling more than 780 mi (1,260 km) away was gray, and for days the air smelled of acidic chemicals. The gases and dust from the eruption blocked some of the Sun's light and heat. Even when the cloud was too thin to see, it was still having this effect. As a result of the Tambora eruption, the whole world cooled down by 0.9°F (0.5°C)— a phenomenon known as a volcanic winter.

THE YEAR WITHOUT A SUMMER

The following year was known as the Year Without a Summer. After a hard winter, frosty conditions continued in the Northern Hemisphere well into spring, meaning that few crops could be sown. There was famine in China, with floods caused by heavy rain. In North America, the spring skies were hazy, and snow and frost in the summer meant that most crops failed. In Europe, failed harvests led to food shortages and riots.

KRAKATAU

At the start of 1883, Krakatau was a mountainous island between Java and Sumatra in Indonesia. It had three craters on its steep slopes. In May of that year, the craters started to spew out clouds of ash, and over the next few months the clouds got thicker and darker, and rumbles could be heard coming from the mountain. At 10:02 a.m. on August 27, the whole mountain exploded. The seabed gave way and most of the island of Krakatau fell into a deep caldera beneath. When the dust settled, two-thirds of the island was gone!

NAME: KRAKATAU

COUNTRY: INDONESIA

TYPE: CALDERA

HEIGHT: 935 FT (285 M)

LAST ERUPTION: 2023

NUMBER OF KNOWN ERUPTIONS: 57

BIGGEST ERUPTION: 1883

PEOPLE LIVING WITHIN 20 MI: OVER 8,000

CLAIM TO FAME: MADE THE LOUDEST NOISE IN HISTORY

Indonesia

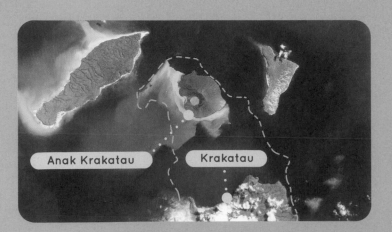

Anak Krakatau   Krakatau

A BIG BANG

The 1883 eruption was 10,000 times more powerful than the largest bomb ever made, and the explosion could be heard in Australia and Mauritius, thousands of miles away. A tsunami 100 ft (30 m) high hit the mainland of Asia and was detected all over the world—even changing the tides in the English Channel! Historians think that 36,000 people were killed by the eruption and the tsunami, including every single person on the nearby island of Sebesi.

RED SKY AT NIGHT

The ash cloud from Krakatau's 1883 eruption spread around the whole world. The specks of dust stayed in the sky for years afterward and created odd effects in the sky, such as making the Moon appear green or blue. Sunlight shining through the ash also produced beautiful blood-red sunsets. It is thought that *The Scream*, a famous painting by Edvard Munch, shows one of these sunsets over Norway at the time.

CHANGING THE WEATHER

During the eruption a cloud of rock and dust was thrown out that went 80 km (50 miles) into the sky. The eruption released 6 cubic mi (25 cubic km) of dust and ash, which is enough to make 10,000 Great Pyramids. The volcano's cloud changed Earth's weather, making the whole world about 1°F (0.6°C) colder than usual for at least a year.

ANAK KRAKATAU

After the 1883 eruption there remained a patch of sea surrounded by three islands. In 1927 an undersea eruption occurred in the middle of this lagoon, forming a new island called Anak Krakatau, which means "child of Krakatau." The young volcano is very active. A big eruption in 2018 caused a large tsunami. Thanks to the warning systems now in place, most people escaped, but thousands of homes were destroyed.

Anak Krakatau

Before 1883

After 1927

KAWAH IJEN

We are used to seeing volcanoes glow with a fierce red color, but at the other end of Java lies Kawah Ijen, a strange volcano that produces blue flames during eruptions. There is a bright blue lake in its crater, but don't be tempted to swim, as it's not fresh water but hot acid! The volcano produces sulfur gas, which burns in the air. At night, the deep blue flames of the burning gas can be seen as they ripple down the mountain!

PINATUBO

This volcano in the northern Philippines had been a quiet place for as far back as anyone could remember. But in 1991, the jungles around Pinatubo were blasted by the largest eruption in living memory! Over a million people lived in the surrounding area, but luckily volcanologists were watching the mountain and realized what was about to happen. The local area was evacuated, saving people from the scorching pyroclastic flow that spread across the area.

. . . .

NAME: PINATUBO

COUNTRY: PHILIPPINES

TYPE: STRATOVOLCANO

HEIGHT: 4,875 FT (1,486 M)

LAST ERUPTION: 2021

NUMBER OF KNOWN ERUPTIONS: 9

BIGGEST ERUPTION: 1991

Philippines

PEOPLE LIVING WITHIN 20 MI: OVER 1,150,000

CLAIM TO FAME: THE WORLD'S LARGEST ERUPTION IN THE LAST 100 YEARS

. . . .

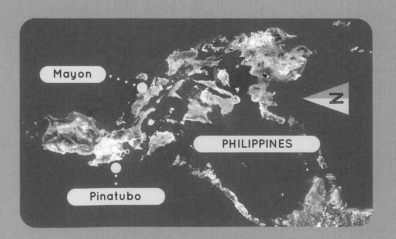

Mayon

PHILIPPINES

N

Pinatubo

EARLY WARNINGS

In April 1991, Pinatubo began to blast out clouds of ash and rock. Volcanologists from across the world came to study it. They recorded earthquakes and a growing bulge near the top of the mountain. Over the next few weeks, Pinatubo became more active. People living there began to leave, and the evacuation zone was enlarged. By June 7, anyone living within 25 mi (40 km) of Pinatubo had been asked to go. About 60,000 people left their homes—and only just in time.

MAYON

Pinatubo is not the most active volcano in the Philippines. About 250 mi (400 km) to the south is Mount Mayon. This volcano has erupted 61 times in the last 500 years. Even so, most of these eruptions are small and tourists come to visit Mayon because it is thought to be one of the most beautiful volcanoes on Earth. The gently curved sides make a near-perfect cone, which is often lit up with lava flows.

A HIDDEN TURTLE The name Pinatubo means "a place where anything grows"—probably a reference to the fertile, ash-rich soils. Local legends told of a terrible sea spirit called Bacobaco who turned into a giant fire-breathing turtle to escape hunters. The turtle fled up the mountain and dug a big hole in the top to hide inside, throwing out rocks, dust clouds, and fire. The monster's howls made the ground shake. This story may have been based on an eruption in around 1450.

WHAT HAPPENED NEXT?

The dark cloud blocked out the Sun and made the area fall into darkness for 36 hours. The eruption had thrown out 1.2 cubic mi (5 cubic km) of ash, making it half the size of the Krakatau disaster. Although roughly 850 people were killed, it could have been much worse without the early evacuation warnings. Many of those sadly killed were trapped in the floods caused by the typhoon. Today, Pinatubo is quiet and a lake has formed in the crater.

BOOM TIME

On June 12, the crater released a column of smoke and dust that reached 12.5 mi (20 km) into the sky. Lightning filled the swirling dark cloud, and pyroclastic flows surged down the mountain. Three days later the summit of Pinatubo collapsed, creating a new crater 1.6 miles (2.5 km) wide. The ash cloud had continued to grow, and pyroclastic flows were spreading more than 9 m (15 km) from the mountain. To make matters worse, a typhoon struck the area, and its heavy rains mixed with ash to form deadly lahars.

FUJI

Mount Fuji, called Fujisan in Japanese, is one of the world's most famous volcanoes. On a clear day its peak can be seen from the bustling megacity of Tokyo, about 62 mi (100 km) away. Fuji's summit—the highest in Japan—is snow-covered for around half of the year. Every year hundreds of thousands of people visit Fuji, and its symmetrical cone shape often appears in Japanese art. The volcano's last big eruption was 300 years ago, but experts say it will erupt again.

NAME: FUJI

COUNTRY: JAPAN

TYPE: STRATOVOLCANO

HEIGHT: 12,388 FT (3,776 M)

LAST ERUPTION: 1855

NUMBER OF KNOWN ERUPTIONS: 58

BIGGEST ERUPTION: 1707

Japan

PEOPLE LIVING WITHIN 20 MI: OVER 900,000

CLAIM TO FAME: LARGEST MOUNTAIN IN JAPAN

Mount Fuji

JAPAN

TOURIST TRAIL

Hikers can climb to the top of Fuji in the warmer summer months, when the snow has melted. The mountain's gentle slope would make it an easy climb if it weren't so big. The sheer scale of the peak means that hikers travel halfway up in buses and then walk the rest of the way. It takes four hours to reach the top, and another four to come back down!

COMPLEX CONE

Japan is one of the most volcanic countries in the world. While the area around Fuji has a history of eruptions going back several million years, Mount Fuji itself is estimated to be 400,000 years old. In fact, it's the third volcano that has stood here. The remains of the other two are buried inside the huge cone. For many years, Fuji had two peaks, but the older one collapsed about 2,500 years ago.

THE HOEI ERUPTION

The last big eruption at Mount Fuji was in 1707. There was no lava, just vast amounts of ash. The ash spread across the eastern part of Japan, covering fields and devastating crops, which caused a famine. The eruption occurred during a time in Japanese history known as the Hoei era. It was a difficult time. Just before the eruption, an earthquake flattened the city of Osaka, and just after it a fire destroyed Kyoto.

SACRED MOUNTAIN

Japan's main religion is Shinto, where people worship the spirits of nature, including those inside volcanoes. There are over 1,000 Shinto shrines at volcanoes around the country, but the most important are at Mount Fuji—the most sacred volcano of all. In summer, people in the nearby town of Yoshida parade through the streets carrying flaming bamboo torches as part of the Yoshida Fire Festival. The festival marks the end of the climbing season and thanks the mountain gods for a successful season.

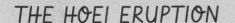

FUTURE ERUPTIONS

Volcanologists have discovered that the pressure of the magma inside Fuji is even higher now than it was during the last eruption. Some worry that a big earthquake near Japan in 2011 may have weakened the mountain, making an eruption even more likely. The people of Japan are well prepared for volcanic eruptions, and everyone living near Fuji has an evacuation plan. However, up to 800,000 people will have to leave. The world's largest city, Tokyo, is not far away. Its population of 37 million people will suffer from the ash fall, water shortages, and power cuts.

KAMCHATKA

The Kamchatka Peninsula is a narrow sliver of land sticking out from eastern Russia. It is a highly volcanic area, with 300 volcanoes—29 of which are highly active. The mountains are covered in snow for eight months of the year, adding to the beautiful scenery. The volcanoes of Kamchatka are protected as a UNESCO World Heritage Site because of the wild landscape and amazing wildlife. Klyuchevskaya is the region's largest volcano.

Russia

NAME: KLYUCHEVSKAYA SOPKA

COUNTRY: RUSSIA

TYPE: STRATOVOLCANO

HEIGHT: 15,597 FT (4,754 M)

LAST ERUPTION: 2023

NUMBER OF KNOWN ERUPTIONS: 109

BIGGEST ERUPTION: 1931

PEOPLE LIVING WITHIN 20 MI: AROUND 300

CLAIM TO FAME: LARGEST VOLCANO IN RUSSIA

Klyuchevskaya Sopka

RUSSIA

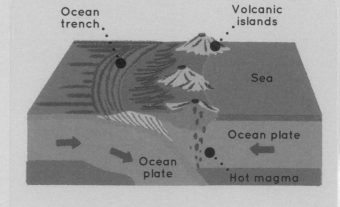

Ocean trench

Volcanic islands

Sea

Ocean plate

Ocean plate

Hot magma

A VOLCANIC ARC

Kamchatka has so many volcanoes because it is on a volcanic arc, where the huge plates that form the Pacific seabed and the landmass of Asia meet. The ocean plate plunges down below the land, forming a deep ocean trench along the east coast of the peninsula. As the two plates slide past each other, hot magma bubbles up, feeding a row of volcanoes that run all the way along the boundary.

KLYUCHEVSKAYA SOPKA

A volcano called Klyuchevskaya Sopka has been erupting on and off at least since 1697, when Russian explorers first visited the area. It's Kamchatka's tallest mountain and also one of the most dangerous to climb. The first group to succeed managed it in 1788. On the next attempt, in 1931, several climbers were killed by lava from a sudden eruption. An expedition in 2022 also ended very badly, with nine climbers killed. It took rescuers two days to reach the three survivors sheltering in a cabin halfway up the mountain.

Karymsky

Kronotsky

VOLCANIC NEIGHBORS

Klyuchevskaya Sopka is not Kamchatka's most active volcano—that title goes to Karymsky. At only 4,964 ft (1,513 m), this mountain is small, but it has been erupting almost constantly since 1996. The eruptions are quite small and release flows of lava and clouds of ash. Not far away is Kronotsky, which is bigger but much quieter, last erupting in 1923. Kronotsky is famous for its almost perfectly pointed cone. No matter where you look from, the mountain has the same shape.

Klyuchevskaya Sopka
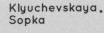

VALLEY OF GEYSERS

Nestled among the volcanic peaks of Kamchatka is a geyser field—the world's second largest, after Yellowstone in the United States. Kamchatka's Valley of Geysers has around 200 geysers as well as many hot springs. The largest geyser, Velikan, shoots spouts of water up to 100 ft (30 m) high! In 2007 a lake formed high up the valley and created a mudslide that filled much of the valley. Many of the geysers were buried but will perhaps erupt again one day.

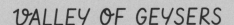

AVACHINSKY AND KORYAKSKY

Kamchatka's largest city is Petropavlovsk, in the south of the peninsula. About 22 mi (35 km) away is a pair of volcanoes called Avachinsky and Koryaksky. Neither of them are very active, producing small eruptions every few decades. However, they are being watched by volcanologists because an eruption here could be very dangerous for a lot of people. Petropavlovsk has grown, and there are 180,000 people living right next to the volcanoes.

MOUNT ST. HELENS

Nestled in the pine-forested mountains of Washington state, this volcano caused the deadliest and most destructive volcanic eruption in the history of the United States. In 1980 the mountain exploded, killing fifty-seven people. Ash from the eruption damaged homes, and the pyroclastic flows destroyed bridges, roads, and railways. After the initial eruption, almost constant smaller eruptions continued until 2008. Mount St. Helens is quiet again, but experts predict that the next eruption will be even bigger.

NAME: MOUNT ST. HELENS

COUNTRY: UNITED STATES

TYPE: STRATOVOLCANO

HEIGHT: 8,363 FT (2,549 M)

LAST ERUPTION: 2008

NUMBER OF KNOWN ERUPTIONS: 40

BIGGEST ERUPTION: 1980

PEOPLE LIVING WITHIN 20 MI: OVER 2,200

CLAIM TO FAME: BIGGEST ERUPTION IN THE HISTORY OF THE UNITED STATES

United States

Mount St. Helens

SHAKY GROUND

Mount St. Helens had not erupted for more than a century, but in the spring of 1980, the area was shaken by a series of earthquakes. These quakes weakened the mountain until eventually its entire north face broke off and slid down. All the rock knocked down trees and swept them into nearby Spirit Lake. To this day, the lake still has logs floating on the surface.

THE CASCADES

Mount St. Helens is one of eighteen volcanoes in the Cascade Range, which runs down the Pacific coast from British Columbia in Canada to northern California in the United States. The volcanoes formed where the Pacific plate is being pushed under the North American plate. More than ten million people live in the area between the Cascade volcanoes and the coast, putting them at risk from the next deadly eruption.

BLASTED SIDEWAYS

The earthquakes were caused by a buildup of lava inside the volcano. Once the outer layer fell, all that lava suddenly erupted, blasting out the side of the mountain. The surge of lava and rock pieces traveled at 220–670 mph (350–1,100 km/h) and left behind a crater 1 mi (1.6 km) wide. Everything within 8 mi (13 km) was killed. The ash cloud created lightning that started forest fires, and the cloud spread east, reaching as far as Oklahoma. When the dust settled, a lot of Mount St. Helens was gone, and the volcano was about 1,300 ft (400 m) shorter.

DANGEROUS NEIGHBORS

Mount Rainier is a little north of Mount St. Helens and almost twice as tall, making it the tallest mountain in the Cascades. It has not erupted for around 500 years, but its summit gets hot enough to melt the snow and ice up there. Mount Rainier is close to Seattle, and more than two million people live within 60 mi (100 km) of it. Another Cascade volcano, Mount Hood, is 50 mi (80 km) from the city of Portland. Both Rainier and Hood are watched closely, in case they erupt like Mount St. Helens.

CRATER LAKE

At the south of the Cascade Range is Crater Lake. Its clear blue waters are contained within a big, round hole—all that remains of Mount Mazama, which collapsed during an eruption 7,700 years ago. Crater Lake has a diameter of 6 mi (9.7 km). At 1,943 ft (592 m) deep, it's the deepest lake in the United States and the ninth deepest in the world.

WASHINGTON

Mount St.
Helens

OREGON

CALIFORNIA

USA

45

HAWAI'I

The biggest and most active volcanoes in the world are on the island of Hawai'i, also called the Big Island. It's part of a long chain of volcanic islands in the middle of the Pacific Ocean. They were formed by lava rising out of the sea, but almost all of their old peaks are now extinct. The Big Island is the youngest area of land, and it contains all but one of the active volcanoes. There are eruptions on the Big Island almost all the time.

NAME: MAUNA LOA

COUNTRY: UNITED STATES

TYPE: SHIELD

HEIGHT: 13,681 FT (4,170 M)

LAST ERUPTION: 2022

NUMBER OF KNOWN ERUPTIONS: 110

BIGGEST ERUPTION: 1868

PEOPLE LIVING WITHIN 20 MI: AROUND 2,000

CLAIM TO FAME: BIGGEST VOLCANO IN THE WORLD

Hawai'i

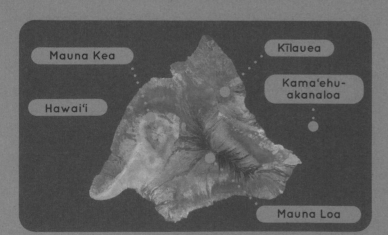

Mauna Kea

Kīlauea

Kamaʻehu-akanaloa

Hawaiʻi

Mauna Loa

WORLD'S TALLEST PEAK

The highest point in Hawai'i is a dormant volcano called Mauna Kea. It is just 125 ft (38 m) taller than nearby Mauna Loa, but that extra height allows it to claim the title of world's tallest mountain! A mountain's prominence is the distance from its base to its peak. Mauna Kea's base is deep down on the seabed, so it has a prominence of 33,501 ft (10,211 m). Although Mount Everest reaches much higher above sea level, its base is also higher, so its prominence is only 29,032 ft (8,849 m).

Mauna Loa

RECORD-BREAKER

Mauna Loa is the largest active volcano in the world. It's not the tallest, but everything else about this mountain is immense. It contains enough rock to fill the Grand Canyon eighteen times over! This rock built up gradually from the lava flows that erupt every few years. As a result, its slopes are gentle but take up about half of the island's land mass. Mauna Loa is not likely to explode like Vesuvius or Pinatubo, but it is still dangerous. In recent eruptions its lava flowed close to the island's main city.

VOG AND LAZE

Volcanoes give the Hawai'ian islands strange weather effects. Vog, or volcanic fog, is created by the smoke and gases released by Kīlauea and other craters. The islands also have laze, or lava haze, which is formed when lava hits the sea. The heat creates a mixture of steam and acids that forms a low-lying cloud. The acid in laze clouds can be deadly.

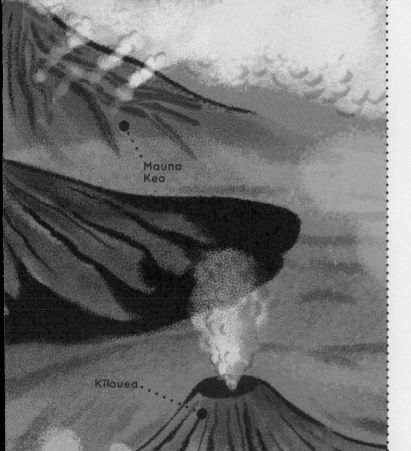

Mauna Kea

Kīlauea

Graffiti art showing Pele, goddess of fire

KĪLAUEA Although it looks like a bulge sticking out of the southeastern slope of Mauna Loa, Kīlauea is actually a separate volcano. Its name means "spewing," and it is the most active volcano in Hawai'i, and potentially on Earth! Hawai'ian legend says that Pele, the goddess of fire, rules the dry southwestern slopes of the island. Kamapua'a, the god of rain, rules the northeast where the climate is wetter. According to legend, constant battles between the two deities have made Kīlauea's crater erupt more or less continuously for the last 200 years.

A NEW ISLAND?

One of Hawai'i's volcanoes has a crater that's about 3,200 ft (975 m) beneath the waves! Although the Kama'ehuakanaloa Seamount is Hawai'i's newest vent, it has probably been around for roughly 400,000 years. It is already 9,800 ft (2,987 m) tall and growing. Scientists predict that it will rise above the waters sometime between 10,000 and 100,000 years from now.

Seamount

Volcanic island

GALÁPAGOS

The Galápagos are located on the Equator in the Pacific Ocean, off the coast of Ecuador. Just like the islands of Hawai'i, the Galápagos islands were created by a volcanic system called a hotspot. The nineteen main islands all began as volcanoes erupting on the seabed, then grew until they rose above the ocean surface to make new areas of dry land. The largest of the active volcanoes is called Wolf. The land-building process is still going on, with younger islands forming the western end of the island chain.

Galápagos

NAME: WOLF

COUNTRY: ECUADOR

TYPE: SHIELD

HEIGHT: 5,610 FT (1,710 M)

LAST ERUPTION: 2022

NUMBER OF KNOWN ERUPTIONS: 16

BIGGEST ERUPTION: 2015

PEOPLE LIVING WITHIN 20 MI: OVER 200

CLAIM TO FAME: HOME TO A RARE SPECIES OF PINK IGUANA

Wolf

GALÁPAGOS

Fernandina Island

Isabela Island

DARWIN'S VISIT

The Galápagos are famous for their unique wildlife, including giant tortoises that can weigh up to 575 lb (260 kg). When Charles Darwin visited the islands in 1835, he studied local animals. What he saw there helped him to develop the theory of evolution by natural selection. This is a very big idea that explains how the great variety of life on Earth, including humans and giant tortoises, arose from older types of life.

A TALE OF TWO ISLANDS

Most of the active volcanoes in the Galápagos are on the islands of Isabela and Fernandina. Isabela is by far the largest island, while Fernandina is the youngest. Isabela is formed from six volcanoes that merged into a single island. Fernandina only has one volcano, called La Cumbre. It has erupted fourteen times in the last fifty years, making it the most active mountain in the region. It's only a little shorter than Wolf over on Isabela.

ERUPTIONS

Scientists have recorded at least sixteen eruptions of Wolf. The biggest was in 2015, and it came after the volcano had been quiet for thirty-three years. Luckily, the lava flowed down the volcano's southern and eastern slopes, keeping the wildlife on the northern slopes from being harmed. La Cumbre has recorded twice as many eruptions in the same period, with the biggest coming in 1968.

VOLCANIC HOTSPOTS

A hotspot like the one that formed the Galápagos has a magma chamber deep below Earth's surface. This magma finds its way through cracks up to the surface, then erupts to make a volcano. However, Earth's crust is always shifting very slowly. After many thousands of years, the volcano is no longer above the hotspot, and it becomes extinct. Instead the hotspot creates a new volcano next to it. After many millions of years, the hotspot will have made a string of volcanoes that are often separate islands.

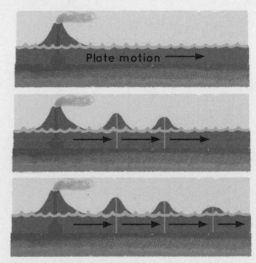

Plate motion

String of volcanoes at a volcanic hotspot

VOLCANO LIZARDS

The Galápagos are home to big lizards called land iguanas, which can grow to up to 5 ft (1.5 m) long. The 200 or so iguanas living on Wolf's northern slopes are pink—though no one knows why! The iguanas on Fernandina are the usual yellowish-brown color, but they have learned to use the volcano's heat. Females climb down into the crater to bury their eggs in the soft volcanic ash. Its temperature is just right for incubating the eggs.

CHIMBORAZO

The country of Ecuador is named after the Spanish name for the Equator, because this imaginary line runs right through it. Ecuador has thirty-six volcanoes, including those on the Galápagos. Ecuador's highest peak, Chimborazo, is the largest of these volcanoes, but it is not the most active. Chimborazo is dormant and hasn't erupted for about 1,500 years, but this vast mountain is still a record-breaker! Its peak is the farthest point on Earth's surface from the center of our planet.

NAME: CHIMBORAZO

COUNTRY: ECUADOR

TYPE: STRATOVOLCANO

HEIGHT: 20,541 FT (6,261 M)

LAST ERUPTION: 550 CE

NUMBER OF KNOWN ERUPTIONS: 6

BIGGEST ERUPTION: OVER 35,000 YEARS AGO

PEOPLE LIVING WITHIN 20 MI: OVER 460,000

CLAIM TO FAME: FARTHEST POINT FROM THE CENTER OF THE EARTH

Ecuador

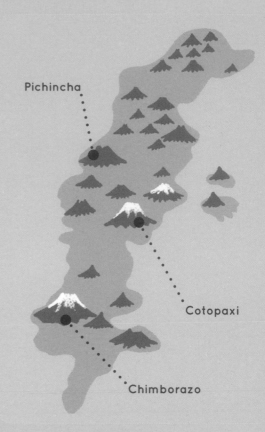

Pichincha

Cotopaxi

Chimborazo

AVENUE OF VOLCANOES

Ten of Ecuador's towering volcanoes form two lines that run north to south through the middle of the country for about 155 mi (250 km). The German explorer Alexander von Humboldt called this area the Avenue of Volcanoes. The five on the western side, including Chimborazo, are mostly inactive. On the eastern side of the "avenue" the mountains are much more active, with some erupting continuously.

Chimborazo

ECUADOR

FARTHEST PEAK

When measured by height above sea level, Chimborazo is nearly 8,530 ft (2,600 m) shorter than Mount Everest. So how can its peak be farther away from the center of the Earth? Chimborazo is very close to the Equator, while Everest is about 1,800 mi (2,900 km) north. Earth's spinning makes the region near the Equator bulge out a little, while the area near the poles is flattened. This means that Chimborazo's base is already farther from the planet's center than Everest's is. Its peak tops out at 3,967 mi (6,384 km) from the center of Earth, more than 1.2 mi (2 km) farther than that of Everest.

SHAPE OF EARTH

This bulging effect is a fairly recent discovery. In the 1730s, the world's scientists could not agree on what shape Earth was. Was our planet shaped like a lemon with pointed poles, or was it more like an orange with flattened tops? To answer this question, scientists took careful measurements in two locations—one near the Equator and one near the Arctic Circle.

COTOPAXI

At 19,393 ft (5,911 m) high, Cotopaxi is one of the highest active volcanoes in the world. It is often covered in snow and during eruptions the biggest dangers are lahars, where melted snow creates a torrent of water that washes house-sized rocks down the mountain. In 1534 a battle on Cotopaxi's slopes between the Spanish and Inca armies was abandoned when the mountain erupted and covered the battlefield in hot ash. In 1744, a team of French scientists witnessed the volcano erupt and destroy the town of Latacunga.

PICHINCHA

A team of French scientists landed in what is now Ecuador in 1736. In order to figure out the shape of the planet, they took measurements on an active volcano called Pichincha. Luckily, the volcano was not erupting at the time. The information that they collected helped to prove that Earth bulges around the Equator.

Lahar damage can bury buildings and destroy whole towns

NEVADO DEL RUIZ

The Equator passes through Colombia, and much of the low-lying land in this area is covered in tropical rainforests. However, the mountain known as Nevado del Ruiz is tall enough to have snow and ice at its peak all year round. It was this snow that made the eruption of 1985 so very deadly. The heat from the volcano melted the snowcap and created a deadly wave of mud and rock that buried a town and killed 25,000 people.

NAME: NEVADO DEL RUIZ

COUNTRY: COLOMBIA

TYPE: STRATOVOLCANO

HEIGHT: 17,320 FT (5,279 M)

LAST ERUPTION: 2023

NUMBER OF KNOWN ERUPTIONS: 20

BIGGEST ERUPTION: 1595

PEOPLE LIVING WITHIN 20 MI: OVER 500,000

CLAIM TO FAME: DEADLIEST ERUPTION IN THE LAST 100 YEARS

Colombia

Nevado del Ruiz

COLOMBIA

A SNOWY MOUNTAIN

Nevado del Ruiz is a complex mountain, covering 77 sq mi (200 sq km) and including several bulging lava domes. The active volcano seen today sits inside a huge caldera left by a much older one. At the top of the mountain is the Arenas crater, which is 0.6 mi (1 km) wide and 787 ft (240 mi) deep. The upper slopes are covered with a layer of ice that can be 165 ft (50 m) thick.

A TRAGIC STORY

In 1985, Nevado del Ruiz had been quiet for about sixty-eight years. It had been even longer—about 400 years—since a big eruption had damaged towns and villages. But at 9 p.m. on November 13, Nevado del Ruiz ejected a cloud of exploded rock 20 mi (30 km) into the sky. It was not an unusually large eruption, but it created pyroclastic flows that melted the ice. That melting released hot water trapped in a temporary lake in the crater, leading to even more melting.

DEADLY NIGHT

Soon a lahar of ice, water, and mud was racing down the mountain, growing larger as it picked up trees and rocks. The town of Armero lies about 46 mi (74 km) from the volcano. The first lahar reached Armero at 11:30 p.m., when most people were in bed. A second hit shortly after. The mud was 130 ft (40 m) deep and flowed through the town for almost an hour. Around two-thirds of the people in the town were killed.

LAND OF VOLCANOES

Nevado del Ruiz is one of sixteen volcanoes in Colombia, most of which are still active. They lie in two ranges—the Cordillera Central, which includes Nevado del Ruiz, and the Cordillera Oriental. The volcanoes in both ranges tower on either side of the wide valley. The Magdalena River flows through it, and its water creates a fertile region of farms and towns. There are also big cities, including the nation's capital, Bogotá. Two-thirds of Colombians live in this river valley.

Nevado
del Ruiz

BOGOTÁ

Magdalena
River

MISSED OPPORTUNITY?

Volcano sensors had picked up big changes in the mountain in September that year, but officials decided that the threat of an eruption was not serious enough to evacuate people living nearby. Local people were not told that their towns were at risk from lahars. Lessons were learned from the Armero tragedy, and governments now take the warnings about eruptions more seriously.

MOUNT PELÉE

This volcano in Martinique sits on an arc of volcanic islands that runs from Puerto Rico to Venezuela. The arc formed where the North American and South American plates get pushed under the Caribbean plate. Mount Pelée is one of the region's most famous volcanoes, but for a tragic reason—its 1902 eruption destroyed an entire city and was the deadliest eruption for the whole of the 20th century.

Martinique

NAME: PELÉE

COUNTRY: FRANCE (MARTINIQUE)

TYPE: STRATOVOLCANO

HEIGHT: 4,501 FT (1,372 M)

LAST ERUPTION: 1932

NUMBER OF KNOWN ERUPTIONS: 54

BIGGEST ERUPTION: 1902

PEOPLE LIVING WITHIN 20 MI: OVER 380,000

CLAIM TO FAME: DEADLIEST ERUPTION OF THE 20TH CENTURY

Pelée

MARTINIQUE

BALD MOUNTAIN

Pelée means "peeled" or "bald," and the mountain was given that name because its steep, rocky sides had few trees or other plants. The plants that did grow here were not helped by the volcano's eruptions, which involved pyroclastic flows that scorched their way down the mountainside. In fact, eruptions with pyroclastic flows like these are now known as Peléan eruptions. Now, the mountain supports luxurious forests.

SMALL DISASTERS

The 1902 eruption of Mount Pelée began in April with a few days of small explosive eruptions, releasing a thick cloud of ash that blocked out the sky and created thunderous lightning. Many people left their villages and headed for the town of Saint-Pierre. But a lahar soon surged down, creating tsunamis when it hit the sea. These waves swept along the coasts, damaging boats and making it harder for people to sail away from the island.

A DEADLY CLOUD

On the night of May 5, the crater of Mount Pelée began to glow—lava was now erupting. On the morning of May 8, a vast cloud of lava and ash sped down the mountain in a blast of hot gases. Within two minutes the cloud had reached Saint-Pierre, 6 mi (10 km) away. Almost all of the 30,000 people in the city were killed by the heat or buried by ash. Later in the month about 2,000 people, who had come to the island to help, were killed in another eruption. The mountain finally fell silent in October.

FAMOUS SURVIVOR

A prisoner named Ludger Sylbaris survived the 1902 eruption because he was locked away in an underground jail cell. It had only a tiny grate in the door, so the room didn't fill with hot dust. Sylbaris was trapped for four days, until rescuers dug him out. He had blocked the grate with his shirt, but the small amount of dust that did get in burned his arms and legs. He later traveled the world as a circus star.

SOUFRIÈRE HILLS

The Soufrière Hills are on the island of Montserrat, north of Martinique. In 1995 this volcano started to erupt in a very similar way to Mount Pelée—but this time scientists sounded a warning. Half of the island was declared a no-go zone and many towns and villages were evacuated, including the capital city, Plymouth. It was a good decision! Within a year much of the emptied area had been covered with ash, and Plymouth was destroyed by a pyroclastic flow. Two-thirds of the islanders left for good.

POPOCATÉPETL

This volcano towers over Mexico City—Mexico's capital and the largest city in all of North America. Its name means "smoking mountain" in the language of the Aztec people who once ruled here. Their capital, Tenochtitlan, was also in the shadow of this great mountain. Popocatépetl lives up to its name because it has had many slow but continuous eruptions in the last 100 years.

NAME: POPOCATÉPETL

COUNTRY: MEXICO

TYPE: STRATOVOLCANO

HEIGHT: 17,694 FT (5,393 M)

LAST ERUPTION: CONTINUOUSLY ERUPTING SINCE 2005

NUMBER OF KNOWN ERUPTIONS: 41

BIGGEST ERUPTION: AROUND 200 BCE

PEOPLE LIVING WITHIN 20 MI: OVER 630,000

CLAIM TO FAME: NORTH AMERICA'S SECOND-TALLEST VOLCANO

Mexico

Iztaccíhuatl

Pico de Orizaba

Popocatépetl

MEXICO

QUIET NEIGHBOR

Iztaccíhuatl lies about 9 mi (15 km) to the north of Popocatépetl. At 17,159 ft (5,230 m), it is the third-tallest mountain in Mexico. Although Iztaccíhuatl is a little shorter than its neighbor, it is wider, and the local people think they can make out the shape of a sleeping woman among its peaks and ridges. In volcanic terms, Iztaccíhuatl is certainly asleep! It hasn"t erupted for 11,000 years and may be extinct.

Iztaccíhuatl

LOS VOLCANES BIOSPHERE RESERVE

Popocatépetl is at the heart of a biosphere reserve set up by the United Nations to preserve the special wildlife in this area. This part of Mexico marks the place where the wildlife of North America meets the wildlife of the tropics. The boundary is marked by a line of forests dominated by a tree known as the oyamel or sacred fir. The animals here include the volcano rabbit and volcano mouse, which live only on the slopes of Popocatépetl, Iztaccíhuatl, and the surrounding area.

THREE MOUNTAINS IN ONE

Popocatépetl is actually the third volcano to exist in this location. Around 200,000 years ago, the first volcano (called Nexpayantla) collapsed during a huge eruption, forming a caldera. A second mountain, El Fraile (meaning "the monk"), formed in its place. El Fraile collapsed around 50,000 years ago, making way for Popocatépetl. However, around 23,000 years ago, one side of the young Popocatépetl exploded, creating a landslide that traveled for 43 mi (70 km). Since then the mountain has grown ever taller.

Popocatépetl

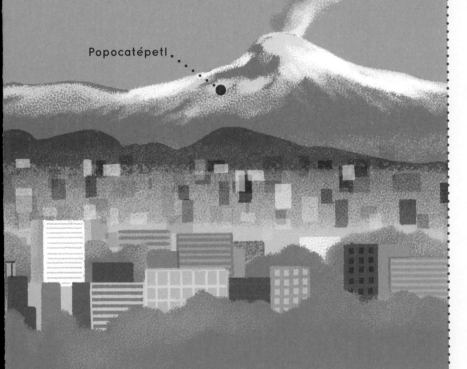

PICO DE ORIZABA

The tallest mountain in Mexico is another volcano, Pico de Orizaba, which stands at 18,255 ft (5,564 m). This peak is about 60 mi (100 km) east of the twin peaks of Iztaccíhuatl and Popocatépetl, near the old city of Orizaba. Pico de Orizaba last erupted in 1846 but often goes centuries with no volcanic activity. Its last big eruption was more than 4,000 years ago.

THE LEGEND OF IZTACCÍHUATL

Close by Popocatépetl is the twin peak of Iztaccíhuatl, with a name meaning "white woman." The covering of snow on its peak makes this name appropriate, but there is also an Aztec myth about a princess called Iztaccíhuatl. She fell in love with Popocatépetl, a lowly warrior. The emperor sent Popocatépetl to war, expecting him to be killed. When Iztaccíhuatl heard her great love was dead, she died of grief. But Popocatépetl was still alive, and he returned to kneel beside her body. The pair were covered in snow and turned into stone, and they remain there today.

SUPER-VOLCANO

A supervolcano is a volcano that has produced an eruption with the highest VEI score of 8. An eruption that big would throw out more than 240 cubic mi (1,000 cubic km) of hot rock and ash—enough to fill 400 million Olympic swimming pools! The most recent eruption this big was in what is now the town of Taupo in New Zealand 26,500 years ago, when mammoths roamed Earth. Somewhere, someday, another supervolcano will erupt. One of the places where this is most likely is Yellowstone in the United States.

NAME: YELLOWSTONE CALDERA

COUNTRY: UNITED STATES

TYPE: SUPERVOLCANO

HEIGHT: 9,203 FT (2,805 M)

LAST ERUPTION: 640,000 YEARS AGO

NUMBER OF KNOWN ERUPTIONS: 3

BIGGEST ERUPTION: 2.1 MILLION YEARS AGO

PEOPLE LIVING WITHIN 20 MI: OVER 200

CLAIM TO FAME: ONE OF THE LARGEST VOLCANOES IN HISTORY

United States

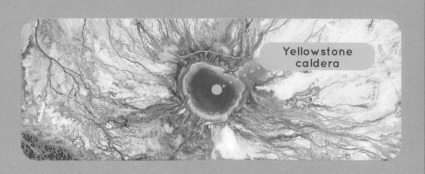

Yellowstone caldera

THE BIGGEST OF ALL

Lake Toba lies high in the hills of northern Sumatra, and this quiet place is the site of the largest-ever supervolcano eruption. The eruption happened about 75,000 years ago and may have nearly wiped out our early human ancestors. The vast explosion threw out about 910 cubic mi (3,800 cubic km) of material—enough to fill in the Grand Canyon three times over! Scientists think that the volcanic cloud cooled the planet for a thousand years, making Africa a desert and reducing the population of our species to just a few thousand.

AMAZING LANDSCAPE

Countries set up national parks to protect their natural wonders for future generations. The very first one was Yellowstone in the United States, which opened in 1872. The area is filled with mountains, lakes, waterfalls, and prairies, but it is also highly volcanic deep underground. There are hydrothermal features such as mudpots, geysers, and hot springs filled with colorful waters.

HIDDEN CALDERAS

There is a volcanic hotspot deep beneath Yellowstone, and it has created three supervolcanoes in this area, each of which have left calderas behind. The biggest eruption, about 2.1 million years ago, formed the Island Park Caldera. The ash from this eruption has been found in rocks about 1,250 mi (2,000 km) away! The last eruption at Yellowstone was 640,000 years ago. This time the ash cloud reached the Gulf of Mexico.

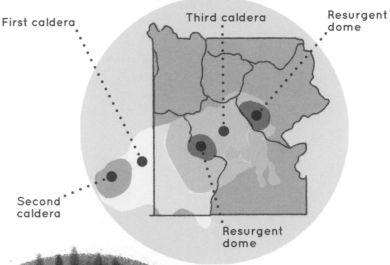

First caldera

Third caldera

Resurgent dome

Second caldera

Resurgent dome

Yellowstone's three calderas

WHAT IF?

A VEI 8 eruption at Yellowstone would be catastrophic. A month-long eruption could spread a thin layer of ash as far as Miami, Florida—more than 2,485 mi (4,000 km) away. The nearest big city, Salt Lake City, would be covered by a much thicker blanket of ash, up to 20 in (50 cm) deep. The ash would bury towns, block roads, and destroy the electricity and water systems for millions of people.

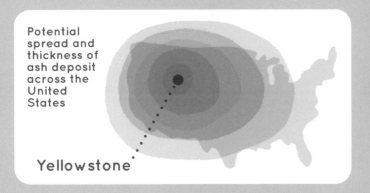

Potential spread and thickness of ash deposit across the United States

Yellowstone

KEEPING WATCH

The calderas at Yellowstone are closely watched by scientists from the Yellowstone Volcano Observatory. They have found areas of bulging ground in the lowland areas near the middle of the park. However, experts say that a new caldera may never form here, and if it did it might not be for another 100,000 years. On top of that, eruptions here are not always immense. In short, the risks of a supervolcano eruption here are very low—but it might happen one day!

OLD VOLCANOES

Once a volcano becomes extinct, its days are numbered. Mountains made of ash and lava are quite soft and unstable, so wind and rain gradually break up the rock until the old volcano erodes away. Many volcanoes become extinct when the lava in their fissure cools, creating a solid plug that cuts it off from the liquid magma deeper down. After millions of years all that remains of some volcanoes is this plug of hard stone—and you'll find them in some surprising places!

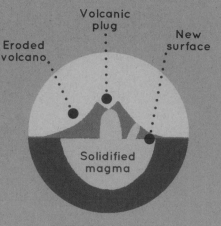

Eroded volcano

Volcanic plug

New surface

Solidified magma

EXTINCT VOLCANO

CITY OF VOLCANOES

Auckland is the largest city in New Zealand, home to more than 1.6 million people. Most of the modern city center is built on ancient lava flows, and the city is home to fifty-three extinct craters. Many of them can be seen around the city as small cones in parks. Volcanologists say that these kinds of craters only ever erupt once, and the most recent eruption here was around 600 years ago. However, the Auckland Volcanic Field is only dormant, and so the experts watch it carefully.

GIANT'S CAUSEWAY, NORTHERN IRELAND

This world-famous rock formation is made from hexagons of rock that fit together as if by design. Legend has it that the Giant's Causeway was used by an Irish giant to cross the Irish Sea to Scotland and fight a rival. However, the formation is completely natural. it was made by a deep lava lake that formed here fifty-five million years ago. As the lava cooled into rock, it shrank a little. It cracked up into six-sided columns that have gradually been eroded away.

BALL'S PYRAMID, AUSTRALIA

Standing tall above the sea, this spiky triangular mountain is off the east coast of Australia, far out in the Pacific Ocean. Ball's Pyramid is about six million years old and is all that is left of a shield volcano that once formed an island. At 1,844 ft (562 m) high, Ball's Pyramid is the world's biggest sea stack—and taller than any skyscraper in New York!

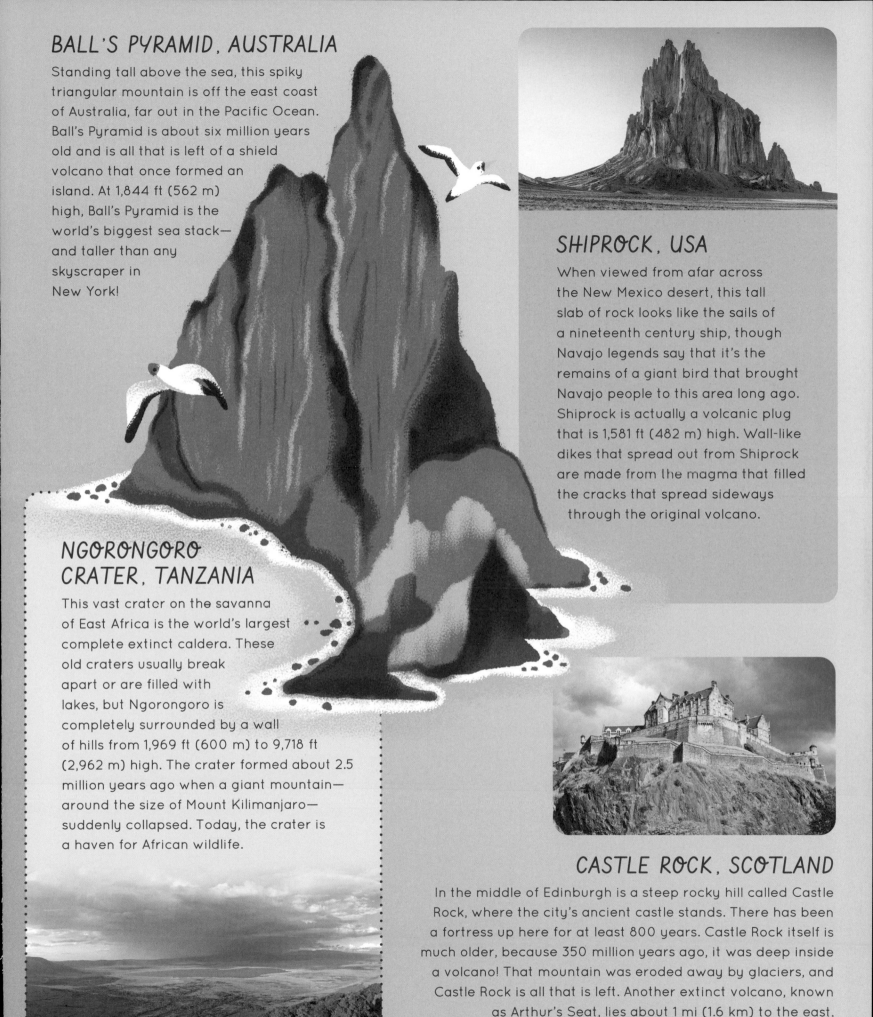

SHIPROCK, USA

When viewed from afar across the New Mexico desert, this tall slab of rock looks like the sails of a nineteenth century ship, though Navajo legends say that it's the remains of a giant bird that brought Navajo people to this area long ago. Shiprock is actually a volcanic plug that is 1,581 ft (482 m) high. Wall-like dikes that spread out from Shiprock are made from the magma that filled the cracks that spread sideways through the original volcano.

NGORONGORO CRATER, TANZANIA

This vast crater on the savanna of East Africa is the world's largest complete extinct caldera. These old craters usually break apart or are filled with lakes, but Ngorongoro is completely surrounded by a wall of hills from 1,969 ft (600 m) to 9,718 ft (2,962 m) high. The crater formed about 2.5 million years ago when a giant mountain—around the size of Mount Kilimanjaro—suddenly collapsed. Today, the crater is a haven for African wildlife.

CASTLE ROCK, SCOTLAND

In the middle of Edinburgh is a steep rocky hill called Castle Rock, where the city's ancient castle stands. There has been a fortress up here for at least 800 years. Castle Rock itself is much older, because 350 million years ago, it was deep inside a volcano! That mountain was eroded away by glaciers, and Castle Rock is all that is left. Another extinct volcano, known as Arthur's Seat, lies about 1 mi (1.6 km) to the east.

GLOSSARY

acidic

Describing a substance made up of acid with a pH level below 7. Acidic chemicals can attack other substances, eating away at them.

active

Describes a volcano that is erupting or may erupt soon.

alpine

Referring to a high mountainous environment.

Arctic Circle

A line around Earth near the North Pole. Above the Arctic Circle the Sun can set all day during winter and stay up all day during summer.

astronomical

To do with the study of stars and the universe.

atmospheric pressure

The weight of the air pressing down from above.

bacteria

A group of tiny organisms that can only be seen through a microscope. Bacteria live everywhere on Earth and are found on and inside the body, especially the stomach. Some bacteria cause disease but others are helpful with digestion.

caldera

A large crater created when a volcano collapses into a magma chamber underneath.

conduit

The pipe that connects the crater to the magma chamber.

crater

The hole left by an erupting volcano.

depression

A low-lying hollow area that is below the land around it.

dike

A mass of volcanic rock that cuts through older types of rock.

dormant

Describing a volcano that has not been active for a long time but which may erupt again one day.

ecosystem

A group of plants, animals, and other organisms that share the same habitat and rely on each other to survive.

Equator

A line around the middle of the planet that divides Earth into two equal parts, or hemispheres.

eruption

When a volcano releases lava, ash, rocks, and smoke—sometimes explosively.

explosivity

Refers to how powerful an eruption is.

extinct

The term for volcanoes that are not expected to erupt again.

fumaroles

Small chimneys on a volcano, where smoke and hot gases escape.

geothermal

Referring to the natural heat from deep inside Earth.

geyser

A natural fountain that gushes out a spout of hot water from time to time.

glacier

A mass of ice that covers a mountain or fills a valley and moves downhill slowly. New ice forms at the top while older ice melts away near the bottom.

hemisphere

Referring to half of a sphere, specifically the division of Earth into northern and southern halves by the equator.

hydrothermal

Refers to water heated by hot rocks underground.

lahar

When a volcano melts snow and ice and creates a temporary river or mudslide.

lava

The name for melted rock that erupts from a volcano.

magma

Melted rock deep underground.

microclimate

Weather conditions, such as high rainfall, that are found in just a small area, which are different from the surrounding region.

mineral

A naturally occurring solid material. Examples of minerals include diamonds, quartz, and iron ore.

observatory

A place containing a telescope and other scientific equipment where scientists can study planet Earth and the universe.

population

A group of animals or plants. Often a species exists as several separate populations.

pyroclastic flow

A high-speed surge of hot gas and dust that flows down a mountain, killing everything in its path.

tectonic plate

A section of Earth's crust.

temperature

A measure of how much heat is in a substance.

tsunami

A large wave caused by an earthquake on the seabed or by large amounts of rock falling into the sea during a volcanic eruption.

vent

The opening on the volcano through which lava erupts.

INDEX

PICTURE CREDITS

ALAMY:

p8tr Granger Historical Picture Archive, p8tr Science History Images, p8mr Sueddeutsche Zeitung Photo, p8br GL Archive, p8br Granger Historical Picture Archive, p11 GL Archive, p20 Pictorial Press Ltd, p24 Science History Images, p28 Scenics & Science, p56 Pictorial Press Ltd.

GETTY:

p35 Wichita Eagle, p47 Walter Geiersperger.

SHUTTERSTOCK:

p9 Natalia van D, p14 a. v. ley, p15 Art_rich, p32 Mark Brandon, p37 Willian Cushman, p41 2013 Lefteris Papaulakis, p51 Natalia van D, p52 AKKHARAT JARUSILAWONG.

DREAMSTIME:

p8bl Servickuz

Words in **bold** are explained in the glossary on page 62.